CATS
OF MARTHA'S VINEYARD
101 ISLAND TALES

LYNN CHRISTOFFERS

MARTHA'S VINEYARD
MASSACHUSETTS

TO ALL THE CATS OF
MARTHA'S VINEYARD

Copyright © 2013 Lynn Christoffers
P.O. Box 3077
West Tisbury, MA 02575
www.lynnchristoffers.com

Library of Congress Control Number:
2013910802

ISBN: 978-0-615-81991-4

Distributed by Vineyard Stories
info@vineyardstories.com
(508) 221-2338
www.vineyardstories.com

Printed in China

Title page: Jasmine with Sadie and Kendra, North Tabor Farm. Above: Daphne

CONTENTS

INTRODUCTION

*I saw cats – tomcats, Mary Ann cats, long-tailed cats,
bobtailed cats, blind cats, one-eyed cats, walleyed cats,
cross-eyed cats, gray cats, black cats, white cats, yellow
cats, striped cats, spotted cats, tame cats, wild cats,
singed cats, individual cats, groups of cats, platoons of
cats, companies of cats, regiments of cats, armies of cats,
multitudes of cats, millions of cats, and all of them sleek,
fat, lazy, and sound asleep.*

—Mark Twain
Roughing It

Prince
(Jan Van Riper, page 105)

Cats are my special friends. I haven't had a foe yet in my travels and Martha's Vineyard cats have been particularly obliging. My secret is that I tell them how smart and special they are: how handsome, how beautiful. Certainly they are for me. In my work, each cat becomes a star. It's a mutual respect and admiration session that takes place. We have that direct connection that clicks. Once we meet it's unconditional love – they shine for my camera.

Priscilla

Photographing cats on Martha's Vineyard began for me the summer of 1989 when I brought my kitten Priscilla to a small camp on Lobsterville Road in Gay Head, set back along a wide expanse of Vineyard Sound. We walked over the sand on long wooden planks through the tall sea grass to get to the house. One late afternoon I photographed Priscilla as she stood in the opening of the red, rusty screen door of the cottage, peering out, showing off her sparkling green eyes. She was scouting the hunt, her gaze turned to the high grass where all kinds of splendid creatures waited.

The following summer I returned to the little camp on the sound, with Priscilla and Bee, a second cat that was a gift from my sister and family. The cats immediately adapted to their new locale, roaming among the beach plum bushes, hiding in the tall grass, or hunting down field mice that peeked out from the rafters of the bunk bedroom. Out of the city shadows, it was their time to explore the wild outdoors – and mine as well. I soon learned that *play* is an essential cat life lesson. No running water, no television or internet, but I had my cameras (still and video) with that special crisp Vineyard light, the sounds of the sea and the Island gulls, and my favorite models: the cats, with their slow, repetitive movement of cats cleaning in the sun. For a few weeks during each of the next fifteen summers, we left my tiny West Village apartment in New York City to spend time at the camp on Lobsterville.

My cat friendships for this book began later when I was fortunate to rent a small cottage on the grounds of the historic Cleaveland House in West Tisbury, the home of mystery writer Cynthia Riggs and her grand marmalade cat, Miss Britty. That was July 2005, and life on the Vineyard beckoned me even more. Soon I was spending parts of the fall and winter on the Island. At that time I still had Bee, who didn't seem to bother Miss Britty. Both cats were my models, and as I settled into Island life, I began to photograph other cats, meeting them and their owners, sometimes neighbors or friends of friends. One cat would soon lead me to another cat family – the cats would introduce me to their people. My

cat portfolio grew, and I found that living in the center of the Island, land-bound rather than with sea view, I was curious to learn what this Vineyard is about, now that I had become a winter resident as well. It was after photographing neighbor Richard Knabel's four prize-winningly handsome Maine coon

cats, in January 2007, that I decided the time had come to make a book of these fabulous creatures.

In *Cats of Martha's Vineyard* you will meet one hundred and one Island families who welcomed me into their homes, farms, offices, shops, barns and fields to get to know their

Lady Diana

resident cats. My goal was to photograph each cat in its natural environment and learn about its habits, its special traits. When possible, I photographed the family group as well. I asked each family to write or tell me something unique about their cat – a short text of their own words. The shared themes from these stories then shaped the chapters of the book. The last chapter is a directory of the cats and owners arranged by town and listing all family members, including other pets.

What have I learned from my six-year journey getting to know cats on Martha's Vineyard? That cats owners are just as diverse as their pets – and each family has a personal story to tell about how their cat became a prominent and integral part of the household. Here the strays, feral half-breeds and cats adopted from shelters stand on equal footing beside the pedigreed felines with papers. It's amazing how many of my cat subjects were adopted from one of the local animal shelters or from an off-Island clinic. No matter what their origin, they are accepted into the family fold and offered the bedroom and best views with no hesitation.

Now I find cats, or they find me, on the Island wherever I go…

-Milky Way in the parking lot at the Chilmark Bank

-Lady Diana in the forest via a shortcut on the way to the high school – a startlingly beautiful seal point Siamese, cleaning her paws and climbing into my car when I stopped to take her photo

-The unknown cat crossing Main Street in Vineyard Haven, out for a mid day jaunt, unafraid of the cars coming and going

-Vercingetorix (Charlie) roaming near the round bales of fresh hay, scouting field mice near Tiasquam Road and looking for neighbor Fred Waitzkin to give him some special stroking

-Miss Daphne rolling in the drive at the Cleaveland House, waiting at my parking spot for me to come home

I soon realized, of course, that I have been making Island friendships as well as collecting feline friends. I hear about crazy cat antics, aging cats and their health issues, the loss of dear pets, and the excitement of new kitties joining the household. In these six years, I've become immersed in the Vineyard's community ways and traditions and daily life, thanks in large part to my cat family friendships. And the cycle does continue: there are new kittens at Mermaid Farm. New stories unfold as we welcome more cats into our lives on Martha's Vineyard – a never-ending source of delight and fascination.

Ginger's kittens

BEGINNINGS

The babies have to be touched, or they'll turn out feral.
Wrap them in a towel, hold them until they purr.

—Lee Dubin

Ginger and kittens with Allen Healy

MISS BIANCA, BUCK, ROSIE, TRAVELER, WEASEL, ZINNIA, GINGER & THREE KITTENS

Mermaid Farm & Dairy
Caitlin Jones & Allen Healy
Everett & Kent

CHILMARK

Miss Bianca Castifiore apparently was born in a stone wall. Teddy, our cat, used to invite her over for dinner when she was a kitten.

Weasel, the red cat, was a stray who was lurking around the West Tisbury dump. He was spotted by eight-year-old Kendra Mills on a nearby property, the old Hillside Farm. Allen was animal control officer at the time, and when he brought him home, we decided to keep him since no one claimed him. The moment Weasel came into the

Weasel with Everett

Miss Bianca

house he dominated the dogs by leaping onto their backs and riding them yelping all through the house. Weasel taught all the other cats how to kill rats. We figured that Weasel must have had a fancy name like Prince Caspian before he became a bush cat.

We got the two kittens Buck and Zinnia from Cynthia Aguilar after Miss Bianca took herself back to the wild to die. I had to put Teddy down at some point and Buck was run over on our own road in August.

Cynthia's daughter Chimele found Rosie in Boston. Rosie ended up having two kittens: Traveler and Ginger. When they were ready she trained them to hunt by stocking the house with dozens of rodents.

After that she was done with being a mother, and moved out back in the greenhouse and barn. Traveler and Ginger grew up with the dog Tex, so they will play with him.

News: Ginger had three kittens in the rain last night!

—Caitlin

Buck with Kent

Ginger's kitten

Zinnia (formerly Tigger)

Tigger with Molly

LUCY & KITTENS: COAL, COW, TIGGER & TURTLE ◆ *Cynthia Aguilar* ◆ VINEYARD HAVEN

Tigger

Tigger, Turtle, Coal and Cow

Lucy and kittens with Cynthia

Daphne with Cynthia

DAPHNE

Cynthia Riggs & Howard Attebery
WEST TISBURY

I never intended to acquire another cat. No cat could ever replace Britty, my mother's marmalade cat, who died at seventeen. But I hadn't counted on the magnetism of a calico tabby kitten at the MSPCA. I'd taken a bed and breakfast guest there as one stop in a sightseeing tour of the Island. I remember distinctly announcing to Jennifer, who was working there at the time, "I'm not here to adopt an animal. I simply wanted Carol to see what a great place this is."

Jennifer reached into a cage and brought out a small handful of fur. "Here's one of a new litter of kittens." And that was it. Within 15 minutes I'd signed adoption papers, handed over a deposit to make sure the kitten would be neutered when the time came, waited long enough for her to have a sesame-seed-size ID inserted under her fur in case she got lost, and there I was, this kitten's person.

Daphne, so named for the wood nymph in Greek mythology, is everything a cat should be: independent, self-satisfied, comical, a great tree climber, a mighty huntress, a good companion, and, at times, a warm blanket.

Daphne

Daphne with Cynthia

DAPHNA, RAISIN & NINE KITTENS

Blackwater Farm
Debby Farber & Alan Cottle

WEST TISBURY

Calico sisters from the same litter, Raisin and Daphna came to the farm at three months old. When they were about a year, they both gave birth to kittens at almost the same time. Raisin had hers first, with Daphna sitting on the edge of the nest, guarding her sister and the newborns. When Daphna, very tired, had her babies a few days later, Raisin helped lick the afterbirth. Together they had nine kittens, all orange and white except one striped tiger. The babies nursed sometimes from one mother, sometimes from the other. Raisin and Daphna were diligent providers: they would catch tiny animals and birds for their kittens. One day the buffet included a duckling, a chipmunk, and a baby bunny laid across the hayloft floor.

—L.C.

Freddy

FREDDY & MOUSE

Stephanie Brothers & Annabelle
WEST TISBURY

We have two cats, brothers, from the same litter. They are both outside, independent hunters who love the Vineyard lifestyle and love climbing trees. But that is where the similarities end. They could not be more different.

Freddy is our striped tiger cat. The last time he was weighed he was 16 lbs. He is a big lump of "freshness"—and I mean that in a good way! He does nothing but lie around the house and "swat" you with his big claws when you go by him. (Hence his full name: Freddy Kruger.) Not to worry — he doesn't mean to hurt you. He just likes the attention.

Mouse is Freddy's brother. He is our black and white tuxedo cat. He is our little independent love bug. He goes outside for a couple days at a time and when he comes home, he goes on one of our beds and sleeps all day. He doesn't mind our dog Cailey joining him on the bed. He absolutely loves the company!

We love them for their different ways. Our family would not be complete without either of them.

—Stephanie

Mouse

Freddy with Annabelle

KITTY

George Morgan

CHILMARK

Kitty was a stray in eastern Pennsylvania who while still a kitten inquired several times at a friend's back door, while ignoring the high pitched screeching of several Maltese terriers inside. Amy, the friend, put food out which Kitty occasionally ate, but she was clearly more interested in getting inside. So the door was left open a crack, this in dead winter, and Kitty marched past the protesting Maltese Guard, inspected the house and then left. She apparently checked out the whole neighborhood in like manner before returning to Amy's door, days later – to stay. She received the name Vashti. No one knows why. Amy spoke about Jane Withers, Elizabeth Taylor's best friend in the film *Giant*, who was saddled with the name.

She loves to have her stomach scratched. As a kitten she'd leap onto the bed, hurl herself on her back waving all paws frantically to attract a pat. More often than not she'd fall off the bed, only to spring back as if on a yoyo.

When Amy died in 2008, she specifically left Kitty to me, knowing that I dislike felines and travel a lot. The name was the first to travel. No more Vashti, and since everyone calls every cat Kitty why not cut to the chase. Then she, like most of her breed, won the new owner over in no time. She let me know early on that she didn't care for me either, so we got along just fine. I give her food, she checks on me three or four times a day to make sure I'm breathing (thus able to continue with the food). As for travel, good fortune led us to a woman she actually likes (and who miraculously likes her back) so a kind of dual ownership has arisen, with Kitty having both a town house in West Tisbury, and a country retreat in Chilmark.

ASTER, GOOSE & MR. NOODLE

Kendra Buresch & Christopher Carroll
Oona Carroll

EDGARTOWN

Goose and Mr. Noodle with Oona and
Kathie Carroll, her grandmother

Aster with Oona

PAWS

Amy & Doug Reese,
Lily Lubin
OAK BLUFFS

From *For the Love of Lily* (a memoir in progress)

By November of Lily's first fall with us, Lily was in love. A little grey ball of fluff with white paws and a white nose had captured her heart. She named him Paws. Lily would tell me how the other kittens wouldn't let Paws get to his food. She told me the story of how he had been found off-island by a little boy who saw a man throw a paper bag from his car onto the train tracks. The boy had ridden his bike over to the paper bag and found it filled with tiny kittens. The boy and his family had taken the kittens to a local animal shelter somewhere in western Massachusetts. I guess they had enough kittens in his town shelter because some of those kittens had been sent to Martha's Vineyard in hopes of a better chance of adoption. Paws was one of those lucky kittens....

■ ■ ■

"Oh my gosh, Lily! Doug got you a kitty!" I cried out. I couldn't believe my eyes. I couldn't believe my husband.

Doug was grinning with pride at his surprise. He stepped out on the porch and brought in a cat crate. Lily ran towards the crate, opened the wire door, and gently pulled a frightened gray kitten from the back of the kennel. "Paws! It's Paws!" She clutched the gray kitten to her chest.

—Amy

PADRAIC JACK (P.J.)

Ann Fielder

WEST TISBURY

Padraic Jack (P.J.) came to us through the great good graces of Ebba Hierta and Chuck Hodgkinson, who rescued him from dogs at Lavender Farm and couldn't keep him because of Chuck's allergies. He was startled the first day by ebullient grandchildren hailing their grandparents, and he scattered. We searched the house, shutting door after door after each search. Three days later and after the town had been alerted to his disappearance we heard a faint "meow" behind one closed door. Shortly after, he went off once more, we thought maybe to hunt for Ebba and Chuck, and we nervously again asked Joan Jenkinson, our town animal control officer, to aid in the search. Some days later, a grandson rushed in to tell us "Your cat is outside."

P.J.'s a Fielder cat now and critically watches the comings and goings of our household, sitting outside on duty until we are all accounted for, as well as keeping rats, squirrels, and rabbits at a safe distance.

PYRO

Dionis & Gary Montrowl

WEST TISBURY

Pyro was found in a dumpster in Aquinnah at about six months. He is a most vocal, affectionate feline and loves to drink out of the faucet.

— Dionis

Pyro with Dionis

Ulla with Eleanor

C.K. DEXTER HAVEN, NEWIE & ULLA

Eleanor Hubbard & Geoffrey White

WEST TISBURY

C.K. Dexter Haven was delivered from Boston the day after Christmas 2010, after living alone in a townhouse following his owner's untimely end.

Extraordinarily green eyes, reminiscent of circular marbles, create headlamps on this tiger's exceptionally rotund girth. By responding to commands, trotting obediently beside his designated humans and generally behaving more like a dog than a traditional independent feline, Dex filled in the gap left by our late Fox Terrier, Peer Gynt. Like Peer, he was equally despised by our two reigning felines, Ulla and Newie who rejoiced when Dexter decided to contribute his tiger hair patina to our son Hubbard's Boston apartment.

After an inglorious 1994 season at the MSPCA, Ulla, a striking calico with aquamarine eyes, was adopted as the result of an illustrated book contract for *The Fisherman and His Wife*. It was supposed to be a strictly professional relationship. Without a second thought, she immediately took charge of our house, our studio, and, in fact, all of Laughing Water. Even at 21, Ulla fearlessly confronts any animal that dares to cross her established boundaries, whether inside of the house or out. Hers is an orderly, discerning, haughty temperament, one that would prefer to see all the lower orders— mice, squirrels, birds—leading productive lives, knitting or crocheting, rather than wandering aimlessly about with no discernible goals. The combination of beauty and an enviable work ethic has made Ulla invaluable as a model. Ulla's image has been on museum and gallery walls, in private collections, and is the subject of a recent film: *Art Imitates Cat*. With über-model Ulla, it surely does.

Newie appeared on our living room sofa on the first day of the new millennium. We know neither her origins nor how she entered the house, but there was no reason to believe her former life had been a bed of catnip. For four long years we were unable to touch or even approach Newie. "Skittish," "wary," "a nervous wreck," all apply to a cat who over time has endeared herself to our family by her very oddness. Even her voice appeared slowly, striking another quirky note: her attempts at meowing sound like the grinding of antique gears. There is a glimmer of hope every now and then when one of us is allowed to sit near or even pet her. On these rare occasions, Newie grimaces and her body tenses, trying hard not to run away while the besotted family member feels like the recipient of a Nobel Prize in Animal Whispering.

Made for cold weather, Newie's cloud gray fur is unusually thick and her fog-like appearance adds to the mysterious persona she projects. Not surprisingly, it is during a snowstorm that this cat's other side appears: she rushes out into the thickest blizzard, leaping wildly in drifts and chasing snowflakes as if they were white catnip.

—Eleanor

Dexter with Geoffrey

33

Newie

Ulla

C.K. Dexter Haven

Dexter

GRACE ◆ *Hermine & Mike Hull* ◆ WEST TISBURY

Mike and I found Grace under a rhododendron bush at my brother Andy's in Redding, Connecticut. We never found out how she got there. It was on my birthday. She was so tiny she fit into my hand. We have had her almost sixteen years now. She has been one of those intrepid, independent cats, six and a half pounds, a great mouser, not very affectionate until she was about twelve. But I have wonderful pictures of her as a kitten playing with my niece, Charlotte, and Caroline Mayhew, when they were little girls. Now Caroline is an attorney in Washington, D.C., and Charlotte is managing a restaurant in San Francisco. And we still have Grace.

—Hermine

RAINBOW

Anna & John Alley

WEST TISBURY

Rainbow came to our house on her own, not liking the home where she was living, which was rented at the time by some people who had several dogs as well as Rainbow. I kept calling the owner to come and get her, and finally got tired of calling him and just started feeding her here. We had no dogs at the time. Our daughter Nicole had a cat, but our son Sam had no cat. At the end of the lease, the renter moved out and came over to say, "Well, the cat is yours now." Sam named her Rainbow (no idea why, he was about five years old at the time, he is now twenty-one). Then Sam, who had wanted a dog for years, finally got a puppy, Star, from the animal shelter here in Edgartown. Rainbow, who really didn't like dogs, was not pleased. She tolerated Star as long as Star remembered her place, always second.

—Anna

37

BOSUN ◆ *Teddie & Ray Ellis* ◆ EDGARTOWN

Nearly 12 years ago, I found a $50 bill in the parking lot at the post office. Ray said, "Let's go out to lunch." Having lost a cat a few months before, I said, "No, let's go to the shelter and see what they have." What we found was Bosun – an eight-week-old kitten whose ears were about as big as his body. He had been brought to the Vineyard with litter-mates from Springfield, Mass. He was the runt of the litter and almost didn't make it across on the boat, we were told. The moral of the story is that if you find money, don't spend it on something fleeting – like lunch. Go get a kitten! Bosun is now 11 1/2 and such a beautiful boy!

— Teddie

Bosun with Ray

NAMING CATS

*Settling on a name for the little guy has seemed to elude us.
When we got him he wasn't anything but an unhappy bit of
gray fluff with a cold...Hey, Little Gray Person.*

—Jeanne Hewett

*His name is Vercingetorix, an heroic leader of the Gauls who
led a great revolt against the Romans; was captured and
killed by Caesar in 46 B.C.*

—Phyllis Méras

Vercingetorix
(Phyllis Méras page 64)

Tigger with Ted

TIGGER & LITTLE TIG

Jeanne & Ted Hewett

EDGARTOWN

Two cats now make up our pet family. Collectively, they are "the Tigs" but separately they are Tigger and – well, Tigger and what? Settling on a name for the little guy has seemed to elude us. When we got him he wasn't anything but an unhappy bit of gray fluff with a cold. Ted had decided our new cat Tigger needed a buddy. Hey, Little Gray Person, we would say. Or B. Box, or Boxer, or Poor Little Fella.

He looked like a box, like the box a cat came in. He stood squarely on his bunch of toes, and was bowlegged besides, and waited to see what was going to bowl him over next. He was all eyes and ears, and not much of a tail. He didn't know how to relax, and spent his first week hiding under radiators and chairs, hunched up in a ball, trying to keep out of the way of the exuberant Tigger, who treated him pretty much as a mouse or a dust ball and batted him about – prey in fact – alternately biting and licking him. It was not easy, being a buddy!

We were on guard all the time, a spray bottle of water or a squirt gun at the ready. Well, all that is past, it's a month later, and our two cats look idyllic on a bench in the sun, grooming each other. They are growing fast. Their play is the most graceful thing to watch—they tumble about, ambush each other with great leaps and twists and roll about doing somersaults, with their jaws firmly locked on each other's throats. It's all just a whisper away from life in the wild, the hold on the

Little Tig

throat, the bites on the back—the early programming remains, and it's all learned in play and used when needed—attacks on small rodents and birds, possibly in turf wars with other cats. I tell my cats, no wars in the neighborhood for you, no lost battles with raccoons—you are day cats, and the gardens and fences and trees are yours, till the sun goes down. They look at me and think their thoughts: "We'll see," they say.

—Jeanne

MOJO

Tommye Brown & Patrick Irwin
Ana & Tom

OAK BLUFFS

Adopted Prince; Night-stalker; Mouse-slayer; Canine-wrangler; Bed-hogger; Dawn-greeter; Chair-warmer; King of Cats. We LOVE You!!

Mojo with Tommye and Tom

VENICE & FLORENCE

Joanie LeLacheur
& Richard Skidmore

AQUINNAH

Our cats' immediate ancestors are Ecuadorian. They arrived on Martha's Vineyard in the belly of their mother! They aren't like any cats I've had before. These cats do not meow; instead they sound more like a crow. They don't purr either but they do wheeze when they are content. And one more special characteristic they have: they wouldn't think to climb down from a tree backwards like any ordinary cat but rather they run down the trunk face front.

Richard said I should mention how much we love them too. We visited them when they were tiny tiny and then we took a trip to Italy and saw them next when they were three weeks old. We chose Venice and Florence at five weeks and brought them home at six weeks. We loved Venice and Florence, Italy, so chose those names for our beautiful kitties.

—Joanie

We first saw them on Valentine's Day, 1998, and have loved them ever since.

—Richard

Venice

45

MIESE

Marie-Louise Rouff & Paul Levine
WEST TISBURY

In early September last fall we first saw this lean cat prowling around our house. Sometimes she followed us but seemed nervous and feral. If we turned around to look at her she would dash off and sometimes run straight up a tree.

It is usually not a good idea to feed a stray cat. If you do the cat becomes yours. We did not feed the cat. We didn't even like her much though she was lean and beautiful. Her fur was a glossy black with a little white bib under her chin. She was too jumpy for our liking and she had a peculiar way of crying aloud. We called her the Moaner.

The cat stayed close. She got into the habit of dashing toward us whenever she saw us come out of the house. She would enthusiastically rub herself against our legs, sometimes nearly tripping us up. We asked around the neighborhood to find out who the owner might be. Some had seen the cat about. Nobody owned her or knew where she came from.

The winter was mild. But then came the January snow. I broke down and put a bowl of cat food outside the pantry door. It was eaten in a flash. The Moaner was now our cat. It took another couple of weeks and quite a few discussions before we let her come inside. After a panicky dash into the house and out again she settled in.

Like the princess in some new fairy tale she changed from a jumpy, feral moaning beast into the most affectionate cuddly pet who likes nothing better than to stretch out on the couch or sit on Paul's lap when he reads. We have named her Miese. In my native language, Luxembourgish, it is the affectionate title we use to address a cat when we don't know its name.

—Marie-Louise

MOON & PHILONEOUS

Mathea & Chioke Morais
Isabella, Delilah & Zora

CHILMARK

Moon with Zora

Philoneous

ZABU

Donald Cronig

VINEYARD HAVEN

The children named him Zabu from *The Lion King*.

ARNO THE GREAT
& BELLA FAIR LADY

Ann Nelson

WEST TISBURY

Who needs romance when you have cats?

Bella Fair Lady

Arno the Great

SCOOBY

Yvette Eastman

AQUINNAH & NEW YORK CITY

That MOUSER! At Yvette's age (99) the shelters won't give her a cat. This one came free. He was so miserable in a New York City storage cellar. We stole him! Yvette loves him, she adores him. He comes with her to the Vineyard every summer. She named him Scooby after my last name.

—Marta Sgubin

DONALD & SIMBA

Marta Sgubin

AQUINNAH & NEW YORK CITY

Donald

The way Donald talks it's like a chirping of a bird, he wants to tell me God knows what!… My cats are very vocal. Since they were very little I've been talking to them, they know the more important words.

—Marta

Caroline Kennedy gave Donald to Marta as a three-month-old kitten. Friends had given Donald to Caroline. She kept him for one month, but was sad to have to give him away because family members were allergic. At least she could visit him at Marta's since she lives across the street in New York City, and at Red Gate Farm when Marta and cats come in the summer to the Vineyard.

Simba, now 12 years old, was adopted as a kitten from a pound in Brooklyn; his birthday is July 15. On Vineyard visits he mostly stays inside, as he is scared when taken outside.

—L.C.

BOB, MAOW-MAOW & WILBUR • *Tobey Roberts* • VINEYARD HAVEN

My cat is named Maow-Maow. I got her from my Aunt Vera who lives in Chilmark. She was a Christmas present and I was eight months old. She was the first stuffed animal I ever liked a lot. I do like real cats and I want one except I can't get one because my dad is allergic. Cats are very snuggly and they can catch mice in your house if you don't want mice.

My Maow-Maow has gone on every single trip I've ever taken except one trip we forgot her and I was very sad inside. We had to get another animal, a Teddy Bear, and I like it, but it's not Maow-Maow. Maow-Maow has lots of friends. One of her friends is named Bob: he is a black and white stuffed cat who sleeps in my bed also. Her kitten is named Wilbur who I also like a lot and he also sleeps in my

bed and Maow sleeps with me of course. Maow-Maow is very cuddly and that is a very special thing about her. At night she helps me go to sleep and she helps her kitten go to sleep too.

I named my cat Maow-Maow and I also named my grandmother Maow-Maow at the same time because I wanted to and because they are both snuggly. And because when I was a baby I thought cats were hilarious especially when they jumped and swished their tails back and forth. That always made me laugh. That's the story of Maow Cat.

Sincerely,
Tobias Henry Lash Roberts, aged six and a half

Wilbur, a Tiger and Maow-Maow with Tobey

FRANKIE & SAM ◆ *Adrianne Ryan* ◆ CHILMARK & NEW YORK CITY

SNICKERS & MILKY WAY ◆ *Betsy Shay* ◆ CHILMARK & BEQUIA, WEST INDIES

MIDNIGHT ◆ *Brookside Farm, Wendy Gimbel* ◆ CHILMARK

Audrey with Barbara and dogs, Charlie & Eddie

AUDREY · *Barbara Moment* · WEST TISBURY

My cat's name is Audrey – after Audrey Hepburn, the actress. Her nickname is Kitty, which is much less formal!

MIDNIGHT, TABATHA & FIVE KITTENS: BLACK DIAMOND, HARLEY, LITTLE MAMA, MITTENS & SUNNY

Penny & Justin Novia,
Tyler & Corey Vanderhoop

AQUINNAH

Five kittens with Tyler and Corey

61

RELATIONS

Every time I see a white cat with black spots on the Island
I think it must be a descendant of Domino's...
After all, in her 17 years she had a total of 136 kittens.

—Phyllis Méras

Poose and Poosa
(Margaret Freydberg page 126)

Jen with Phyllis

JEN & VERCINGETORIX

Phyllis Méras

WEST TISBURY

Jen was found in an apartment parking lot in Chicago and flown to me by the United Airlines employee, Jason Silber who found her. He had initially hoped that his sister, Laura Silber of West Tisbury, would take her, but she couldn't so she suggested me. In making the "sell" by e-mail from Chicago, Jen was described as resembling "a loaf of bread on legs." Which she does since she is gold and white, short-legged and the same shape. When Jen and Jason got to Boston, there was a snowstorm and he had to smuggle her onto a bus because there were no flights to the Vineyard, and then into a motel in Falmouth because there were no boats. When she arrived, she turned out to be vastly overweight at 15 pounds. So it was that six years ago a Chilmark kitten named Vercingetorix joined the ménage to "slim her down" by playing with her. That didn't happen, but both cats remain in the family. They tolerate each other.

—Phyllis

Growing up, Phyllis spent each summer in East Chop with her family. Her father hated cats; her mother liked them. One August day her mother brought home a white kitten with black spots named Butch from the hairdresser in Oak Bluffs. Phyllis changed his name to Domino, and before long the cat surprised the family by giving birth to kittens. Domino lived to be seventeen years old, producing a total of 136 kittens in her lifetime. Young Phyllis carried the kittens in her arms throughout the neighborhood looking for homes. Mothers brought their children indoors when they saw Phyllis coming.

One of her cat takers was the socialist writer, Leo Huberman living in a cottage in Menemsha. Phyllis discovered his identity a year later when, as a cub reporter for the Vineyard Gazette, she was sent to interview him. Opening the door, he blurted out, "You are the girl who gave me that flea-ridden cat with the double paws!" There was Domino's last kitten, born when she was seventeen, now a flea free year- old cat. And of course, showing off his inherited white fur with black spots!

—L.C.

Vercingetorix

Vercingetorix

Jen

Jen

BRUNHILDA, BRULEE, PARFAIT & TOFU

Richard Knabel, James Osmundsen
WEST TISBURY

Tofu

Four cats are all Maine coons.

Brunhilda: female, sister to Tofu (died 2012). Tofu: mother to Brulee & Parfait, white with blue & yellow eye (died 2011). Brulee: brother to Parfait. Parfait: green eyes, silver tabby, biggest: 23 pounds. Brunhilda is the Queen of the house, and lets everyone know it. Over three years she had three litters, a total of 12 kittens, and the last litter was five females. The first two litters all got Wagnerian names. By the third we had run out of Wagnerian characters, so we called the five the "Rhine maidens" Four of them went to a breeder in Pearl River.

The relatives down the street: The elder Maleys got the two surviving kittens from Brunhilda's first litter in 1995, and Ziglinda (renamed Molly) now lives with Corinne Moran of Oak Bluffs. Zigmund, her brother, didn't survive his first year. Suzie Wasserman on Music Street has Zigfried, Ziggy (later renamed Smokey), one of Brunhilda's second litter in 1996, and had Gussy (sister to Brunhilda and Tofu, two years older) who died at 15. Actually, Ziggy was the leader of a pack of four. Brunhilda and Tofu are litter-mates and were born in May 1994. Soufflé is their mother, and looks exactly like Tofu.

—Richard

Suzette, the newest member of this Maine coon cat family is princess of the house. Page 202

Parfait with James

Brunhilda

Brulee with Richard

ZIGGY ◆ *Susan & Robert Wasserman* ◆ WEST TISBURY

MOLLY

Corinne Moran

OAK BLUFFS

Bailey the dog with Corinne

Molly

MOLLY & HER RELATIVES

Parfait, Molly's cousin

Brunhilda, Molly's mother

Ziggy, Molly's half-brother

Molly, daughter of Brunhilda

GUS & OCICATS

Barry Nevin

EDGARTOWN

Barry has ocicats living in her backyard. An ocicat is a Siamese, Abyssinian and American shorthair combination. She gave Kitty Murphy and June Manning their ocicats (all half breeds). Kitty's cat Neizshki was from Barry; the mother cat was Barry's Amanda from a family in Chilmark. The father was a tom cat.

Gus is a part Manx eight-week-old kitten. A little cowboy, he climbs through the open window to get into the house.

Gus

Gus

KATE LIN

June Manning

AQUINNAH

Trina Kingsbury gave us Kate, who she got from Barry Nevin of Edgartown. Part ocicat, Kate was originally for my mother, Jacquelyne. Mother had a good year with Kate – I'd bring her to Windemere to visit once a week. Kate Lin Manning was named Lin for my mother's doctor; Kate for Barry's sister Kate who passed away in 2001.

Kate is very special. She does things that are very unusual for a cat: plays with deer on the front lawn; jumps eight feet; has been skunked twice; comes in out of the rain and gets dried off with the blow dryer and doesn't seem to mind. She poses as if she is a prima ballerina. She has spent her years resting on a double bed upstairs where she enjoyed the southern exposure each day. Of course, she spends her nights at the foot of my bed. That's the bonding the two of us have.

Kate has a boyfriend, Moshup, who looks like her but has a browner face. He is also an ocicat, and belongs to Liz and Ken up Lighthouse Road. The two cats are always wandering off to meet each other.

One day Kate was lost in the woods of Chilmark while we were visiting Trina. She had jumped down from my lap and run into the woods. Trina was concerned and wanted to call the animal control officer. I was not concerned. Four hours later Kate showed up across the pond and meowed and I walked around the pond to rescue her. She obviously had not traveled far and came right back to me.

Tossu and Alice the dog

STAR PIKKU "TOSSU" II ◆ *Trina E. Kingsbury* ◆ CHILMARK

Tossu has me very well trained — these animals boss me around constantly. From the time I got him at eight weeks old, Tossu lived on fresh lobsters and fresh venison my brother brought home. Then at six months old he turned up his nose at both on New Year's Day and never touched them again.

ADAGIO, ZENA, NEIZSHKI, DANDI & LUTEIA

Kitty Murphy

WEST TISBURY

Adagio

Luteia and Dandi

MOSHUP

Elizabeth Witham & Ken Wentworth

AQUINNAH

Before Moshup, we had adopted one of the Vineyard
ocicats that are around the island. His name was Lihai.
After about five years of having Lihai in our lives, he
mysteriously disappeared and we were heartbroken. When
Ken and I got married, my sister Aretha gave us a card
with a picture of a Dyson vacuum cleaner on one side, and
an ocicat on the other, and asked us which one we would
prefer. After some discussion, we decided to go for another
ocicat kitten. He came from Pennsylvania. Aretha, Ken and
I all were at Logan to collect him when he arrived. It was
love at first sight. Moshup is five years old and likes to take
walks with us. He even walks down to the beach with us,
and is a big fan of digging holes and rolling in the sand.

— Liz

KITTY & LOTUS

Aretha Brown & Fiona

CHILMARK

Kitty is the male, Lotus the female. The romance died after one year. Now like an old married couple who are together for convenience only, most of the time they disappear—but are secretly loving each other. Lotus stays in, never goes outside, but when Kitty goes out she cries for him to come back— like some life relationships.

Lotus

Kitty with Fiona

PEARL

Despina & Barney Duane

OAK BLUFFS

Pearl didn't like her owners. She'd walk around the Campground showing up at our doorstep, meow meow!! We fed her and soon she stayed all summer, showing up again the next summer when we came back from Cambridge…

—Despina

I remember feeding Pearl, Dee Duane's white cat on Pequoit Ave., in the off-season, after they went back to Cambridge. They'd leave food out for her, but she would come over to the church looking for more.

—Pastor Marcia Buckley

Zorro with Ella

ZORRO

Pastor Marcia Buckley & Ella Clarke
OAK BLUFFS

Zorro is doing well and is especially fond of my granddaughter Ella. When the kids stay over, Ella loves to let him in the house in the morning and Zorro likes to lie in bed with her.

—Pastor Marcia Buckley

When I come over to my grandma's house, at night Zorro sleeps with me – he puts his head on my pillow! Zorro is the best cat in the whole entire world!!

—Ella

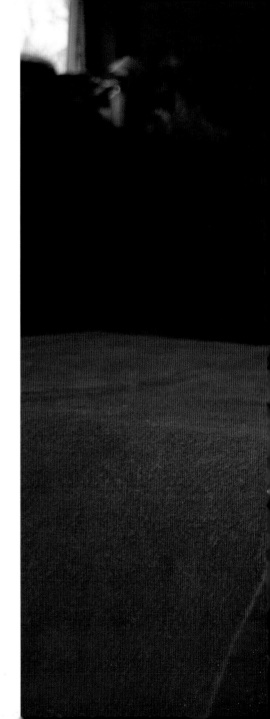

CATS WITH JOBS

*Once we were in the patient's room I would close the door,
Zoe would explore along the perimeters to know the space,
and eventually just jump up on the bed and settle in for some
cozy time. I could leave and come back in an hour or two,
finding patient and cat resting easily. She did more good than
any medicine could ever hope to do!*

—*Juleann VanBelle*

Zoe

ZOE

Juleann VanBelle & Ken Leuchtenmacher

WEST TISBURY

Zoe with dogs Stanley, Molly and Angie

I was working for Hospice of Martha's Vineyard when Zoe came to live with Ken and me, joining our assorted collection of domestic and farm animals.

While at Hospice I had the good fortune to work with Gerry Tailer—one of the original hospice volunteers. She and her husband Peter ran the Windfarm on the Edgartown Road years ago. Gerry and Peter raised rabbits as part of their educational effort. She incorporated them regularly with her hospice clients, bringing them with her simply for the joy of tactile comfort but also as a means to open up the discussion about the cycle of life—they helped bridge the gap to the difficult discussion facing people close to death.

Zoe seemed like a perfect candidate for this kind of exposure as well. Of course, she had a ton of personality—always a flirt and who could resist her big blue eyes? But she also had a natural willingness to travel, an unusual trait in a cat.

So I began to bring her with me to see patients in Windemere, the hospital, and a couple of people at home. It was really rather amazing to just carry her down the hallways—she had no fear, simply relaxing into my arms—no crate for her!—and greeting people along the way. Once we were in the patient's room I would close the door, she would explore along the perimeters to know the space, and eventually just jump up on the bed and settle in for some cozy time. I could leave and come back in an hour or two, finding patient and cat resting easily. She did more good than any medicine could ever hope to do!

Zoe made a difference for three women in particular—each of them having a difficult time, for different reasons. Each of them preferred the company of animals to the company of people. One of them—she never did remember my name—but, if I didn't bring Zoe with me she would say, "Zoe—where is Zoe!" Zoe was the real nurse—I was just to be tolerated.

—Juleann

Zoe with Juleann

BABY CAKES

Sue Tonry

VINEYARD HAVEN

Baby Cakes was born on March 3, 2001 in Brockton, Mass. Eight weeks after his birth he and his mother were brought to the Vineyard. The following Sunday morning I had a dream with him washing his belly sitting on a green grass hill with Lucky, my missing Maine coon, and Bandit, my tuxedo cat. (Baby was born in Brockton the same day Lucky went missing here.)

On Tuesday I drove to the MSPCA in Edgartown and there he was. My little animal soul mate. The kittens were all crowded in one corner of their glass enclosure. Baby was sitting all by himself at the other end pawing at the glass for me. I knew right away he had to come home. This little ball of fur connected with me in a way no other cat in my lifetime had ever done. We were both connected spiritually. By that I mean we could hear each other. Animals sound like people when they can connect to someone who can hear them. I can send him messages by way of thoughts without using vocal words and he does what I ask.

He grew up in the shop on the counter that summer. He also walked around the neighborhood on a leash. When he was six months old and it was springtime I let him go. He returned to places like the Steamship Authority and the workers would call me to say he was there. He soon learned to come home by himself.

For years he would walk on the beach with me on a leash to the amazement of everyone. One day a dog obviously not on a leash attacked him and from that day on he would never walk on the beach again. That was a very sad day in our lives.

Baby Cakes has a special love for working in the shop every summer. I can predict how much business there will be because of him. Whenever he's in the garden off season I have to go find him and tell him, "Someone wants to see you." He winds his way out of the garden and walks in the back door. He waits for me to say, "Run into the shop, they want to see you." Instantly he perks up like he's walking onto the stage—ears up, tail up, shoulders straight—and he runs right for whoever is waiting for him. Giving a head rub and loud meows.

The best thing about Baby Cakes is the joy he gives me every day. He runs to the truck and waits for me to take him for a ride. He has a special seat that puts him up to the dash and allows him to watch where we're going. His special words are, "MOW me" when he wants me to pet his head while we ride. I'm so lucky to have him as my animal soul mate.

PURL & TWIG

Katherine Long

WEST TISBURY

Twig and Purl sleep a lot – like all cats – but these two do their best to stagger their naps so that one of them is always on duty and as close to me as possible.

The "on-duty" cat assumes an air of great responsibility, which is normal for Twig but a very great stretch for Purl who is still very kitten-ish. Nevertheless, when Purl is on duty, she takes it very seriously and follows me while Twig naps.

Both of them have become enthusiastic and rather inefficient mousers. Twig is great at catching mice and parades around the house with mouse in mouth. And poor Purl trots along behind and Twig doesn't let her get close. This can go on for hours.

Eventually either the mouse gets away or Twig lets it go and the whole mouse hunt/parade/catch-release starts over again. Twig doesn't let me close to the mouse either and I see it running around the house when the cats get bored. After a day or so I find a dead mouse on the floor — though with no real signs of what killed it. Exhaustion maybe.

My friend Glenn says that my cats are just too well fed to be interested in actually eating a mouse.

Twig with Katherine

Purl

CHARLOTTE & PHOEBE
Hal Garneau & Dan Waters
WEST TISBURY

From the time they were kittens, we've always planned our lives around Phoebe and Charlotte, and that has always suited them just fine. They eat before we do, they tell us when it's time to play, and when they're having a lap-nap, we can't move unless we apologize profusely. They have many more toys than we do.

The books say that Burmese are "the clowns of the cat world," and there's no doubt that they have a sense of humor. However, they are also natural supervisors. If you ever have a spare minute in your day, they will not hesitate to find a job for you. Usually that job involves giving tummy rubs.

—Dan

Charlotte with Dan

SPOT

Hilary Blocksom & Bill Honey

WEST TISBURY

Spot is a barn cat, and only appears at six am and three pm for her food, when I feed her in the barn. I find her up in the hay mow. She cries for me to bring her down, but she then leaps down herself into the horse manger, landing with a giant thump.

—Bill

WMBC: the World's Most Beautiful Cat

—Hilary

BETTY

Leslie Baker

WEST TISBURY

Betty, looking relaxed and nonchalant, was sitting in the middle of the cat room at the Martha's Vineyard MSPCA when I first saw her. She looked so much like my former cat Nellie, who was the model for my children's book *The Third-Story Cat* (Little, Brown, 1987), that I knew I had to adopt her. Betty shares the house with two border terriers, Zenny and Pancho, and Stella the Bernese, who keep her on her toes. All four of them like to hang around the studio while I work despite the fact that they sometimes wind up wearing blotches of paint on their coats. But they don't seem to care, especially Betty with her calico coat of many colors.

BLUE, CALICO & THOMAS • *Red Pony Farm, Karin Magid* • WEST TISBURY

Thomas with Pip, the horse

Thomas

Blue and Thomas

Calico

CATS
WITH SPECIAL TALENTS

Cats are circumspect.
They have strong emotional connections to humans;
they are "tuned in."

—*Enid Haller*

Milky Way and Snickers
(Betsy Shay page 57)

BESSIE

Tracy Thorpe & Jim Karabees
Thorpe & Kieran
CHILMARK

The remarkable thing about Bessie, which we learned only after Zulu, our other cat, died and Bessie could spend relaxed time with us, is her ability to empathize. When any member of our household is feeling sad, distraught, crying or generally miserable, she comes running. I've even thought to myself, "I wish Bessie were here," and she's come. I've also seen her curled around Thorpe's head at night while he's sleeping, trying to give his long hair a "bath." I guess she has transferred her mothering instinct from the kittens she will never have, to us.

—Tracy

Bessie with Kieran and Thorpe

LILLY • *Martina & Jerome Gonsalves, Adahy & Yannick* • OAK BLUFFS

Since Lilly was a kitty, she's used her paw like a spoon to scoop up her food, then licks her paw clean. Before she eats, she spins the bowl around on the floor. Just before we put the food bowl down, she sits up high on her back legs with her paws in the air. If she's REAL hungry, the higher she goes.

—Jerome

BOY ◆ *Enid Haller & Sam Hiser, Bean Haller-Hiser* ◆ WEST TISBURY

The animals have their own language which we all understand. Boy says, "I want to go out," and we know what he wants. Cats are circumspect. They have strong emotional connections to humans; they are tuned in.

—Enid

BRITTY

Cynthia Riggs

WEST TISBURY

Britty, my mother's marmalade cat, would do somersaults outside the bathroom door while Dionis was inside. "Just a moment please, I'll be right out," she'd say.

PRINCE

Jan Van Riper

VINEYARD HAVEN

Prince is something: he follows me around the house, he is right by my side. When I was disabled from an operation and used an electric chair to get upstairs, Prince figured out how to ride up on the shelf with me.

SMOKEY ◆ *Pamela Danz* ◆ WEST TISBURY & NEW YORK

Shadow the dog greets everyone who comes and often he goes out to the car and walks visitors down the path to the office. Smokey the cat is Shadow's brother. We got him when he was ten weeks old. Smokey learned from Shadow that when you greet people you roll over and have your tummy scratched. Clients get such a smile when they have Smokey walk up to them and he rolls over like his brother.

WHISKERS

Joyce Bowker & Greyson Bowker

EDGARTOWN

Whiskers visited the neighbors down the street and they didn't know his name at first so they called him Charlie Chaplin because of his mustache. But soon they knew his real name when they found out he was my cat.

—Greyson

He sounds like a baby. "No," I say to the neighbors, "don't worry, it's just my cat."

Many times I'll get a call and have to go get him from the police warden at the "Cat House."

I leave my home on Cooke Street to go to the movies and Whiskers will walk with me. When we almost get there, I stop talking to him, hoping he will go back home. But he jumps over the fence and crosses the busy street to the movie theater.

He knows where he'll find me—I'm not saying that he can time the movie, but there he is waiting for me when I come out. We walk home together. He's my daughter's cat.

—Joyce

Whiskers with Greyson

Rosie

ATHENA & ROSIE

Sue Hruby

WEST TISBURY

When I permanently moved to the Vineyard I came because I wanted to be closer to nature. Years of living in New York had left me depleted. I found myself craving a life that would nourish me differently than I had lived. My cats accompanied me. When I moved, Athena (then known as Willow) was an urban cat, two years old. Her arrival on the Vineyard was more than eventful. She was the adventurer. She ate a bee, she got stuck in a tree, she chased the crows, she herded the turkeys. She taught herself to hunt.

I brought Rosie into the family when she was four months and she promptly became the greatest annoyance in Athena's life. Rosie lived her first two years with her only access to the outdoors through her cat pen. One day, that was enough. She let me know she was a big cat now and bulled her way outdoors. I had a choice: I could spend all day trying to keep her in, or she could go out. She went out. Athena taught Rosie to hunt. I spied them from the deck sitting at the brush line about 10 feet apart hunting for mice. Rosie watched Athena, occasionally chasing her tail. She cornered a baby rabbit but was unsure of what to do with it. She escorted it out of the driveway. She came home with a squirrel tail in her mouth looking rather like Groucho Marx.

When Athena was five she broke her hind leg in a hunting adventure and came home in 20-degree weather on a windy night, literally dragging her leg behind her. She spent the winter after surgery mending in front of the bathroom heater. In the

spring when she was healed we went out together, she on a leash. She took me to her hunting spots and I stood waiting with her. I learned to bring a book as we hunted in the field. One day we walked across to the next property close to where I thought the accident had happened. She started chattering, as if she were telling me what had happened. It made me want to know what had happened to my cat that had caused an accident so critical that amputation was an option seriously considered. I found an animal communicator.

Astounding as it may seem I learned things that I knew to be true that this woman could not have known. We changed Willow's name to Athena at my cat's request. She responded to her new name immediately. I was shaken. Maybe there was something to this. To learn what my cats have to say is a profoundly satisfying experience. Maybe I have really become one of those bag-lady type women muttering to herself, leaving crumbs and morsels for the animals. If so, it is immensely gratifying and I am thankful for this experience.

LEO

Catherine Finch

EDGARTOWN

Born at the MSPCA to a small stray, Leo became a big cat.

As a kitten, he plopped fuzzy toys into a bowl of water kept outside for a large, aging black dog who took a daily constitutional through the yard. With focused enthusiasm, little Leo swished those bobbing balls around until the liquid was mostly outside the container. He'd look up, then, from inside the ceramic mixing bowl, a wide-eyed and soggy muddle.

Maturing into a steady, grounded adult, Leo took the job of keeping tabs on our property. To this day, he walks the perimeter of our boot-shaped half-acre lot and checks for anything in need of attention.

After being off-island, I was drafting in my studio one morning, when Leo meowed at the door. He wanted me to follow, so I did. First, he led me to our medicine wheel. Walking from one spot to another, he showed me the innards of a very large bird. Next, he took me to the back of the property, where a wild turkey had been dug up and strewn about, feathers everywhere. Leo clearly wanted the mess cleaned up. I later learned that a housemate had found the dead turkey and buried it, just not deep enough.

During my recent journey with cancer, when I couldn't move from the chemo, Leo stayed by my side day and night, no matter how stifling my upstairs room got from the summer heat. He could've left anytime through his cat door. Then, when I was uncomfortable after surgery, he stayed off the bed until he knew I was healed enough to enjoy his company again. I love my wise and big-hearted friend!

CAT CHARACTERS

*Beebe was the classic bad seed, maybe a sociopath, if such
a thing exists in the feline world. He cuddled up to people
until they gave him their hearts, then he'd sidle down
and bite their legs.*

—Holly Nadler

Mouse
(Stephanie Brothers page 24)

MAC ◆ *Marvene & Bob O'Rourke* ◆ CHAPPAQUIDDICK

My husband simply said, 'Get the damn cat if you want it.'

—Marvene

Mac the Cat and Me: Our relationship started badly. I recall it as a sneak attack. Me, the unsuspecting human. And he, a male coon, a yard long, 15-plus pounds, a crinkled ear, camouflage stripes and probably hungry. This adult cat had spent less than a week in our house after doing time in animal rescue. My wife was off-island, and my job was to fill the feeding dish for the new family member. As I walked through the kitchen shadowed by the cat, the animal leaped at a leg,

which I first shook off as a friendly gesture. However a second claws-out attack from the rear changed my mind as a trickle of blood ran down my leg. Surprised and disoriented, I shoveled out huge amounts of wet and dry food into the feeding tray, sprinkled the floor with cat treats, jumped in my car and headed for the shelter in Edgartown.

"I am here for therapy," I told the supervisor. "I am not a cat person." Her advice was to take charge, point a finger and spit out an angry "bad cat" at the animal. Seeking additional help, I consulted with the Maine Coon Breeders and Fanciers Association for enlightenment.

The breed, I discovered, is one of the oldest natural felines in North America. No surprise, it is the Maine State Cat. Its origin in America, since it resembles the Norwegian Forest cat, may have come on a voyage with the Vikings. It's designed to survive in cold climates. This makes the Chappaquiddick climate ideal for our cat.

Since then I have established a relationship of detente with our cat, friendly enough, but cautious. I infrequently swear at him these days. He has overcome the wintry habits of his Norwegian forebears. He is not a rodent hunter or bird snatcher, has a penchant for warmth and is a barometer of harsh weather, never seeking the woods surrounding our house when the temperature drops or rain is threatening.

I try to scratch his head on occasion as a goodwill gesture, and he does seem to like to hang out with me inside, curling up on my shoes and leaping onto the keyboard of my computer at inconvenient times. So I guess we are OK with each other. However, I do look back over my shoulder as a precautionary measure when Mac the Cat is trailing me, a short lunge and cat's paw distance away from my leg.

—Bob

MAGIC

Jane Seagrave & John Kennedy
WEST TISBURY

Magic's true owner is our daughter, Emily. Born on Halloween, Emily at age eight thought it would be fitting to have a black cat and it was she who named him.

Magic has always been companionable, not cuddly. He loves to be where people are, but prefers to have them seated so he can keep an eye on them. He will at times speak sharply if we try to leave a room or "herd" us back if we try to take a walk.

His favorite game is "Cat in Jail," where he positions himself behind the spindles on a staircase and gently whacks at the legs of people going by. Some of his happiest days were when he was two and lived for a year with us in Lugano, Switzerland. Our home was next door to a vineyard, and Magic would spend hours roving up and down the rows of grapevines stalking lizards.

We sometimes wonder if he thinks he moved to Martha's Vineyard under false pretenses — nary a grape leaf or lizard in sight. At nearly 14, his best hunting days are behind him and he seems largely content to watch the outside world from behind sliding glass doors.

—Jane

BEEBE   ◆   *Holly Nadler*   ◆   OAK BLUFFS

Our Siamese cat followed in the footsteps of the tragic death of his litter-mate, Baby Roo who was the sweetest, most puppy-like kitten imaginable. Beebe was the classic bad seed, maybe a sociopath, if such a thing exists in the feline world. He cuddled up to people until they gave him their hearts, then he'd sidle down and bite their legs. He would also swipe his claw across your arm as he perched on the counter to remind you to rustle up breakfast. When Charlie, my son, was doing homework, I'd hear a roar of "Get off my keyboard!" and the next thing I knew, Beebe would get

pitched through my door to be my problem for the night. And still we kept him. It was love/hate. He did mellow over the years. He presided at my store, Sun Porch Books in Oak Bluffs, for the six years it was in operation (2002-2008). Because he still specialized in cuddling, families made an event out of visiting him in the store after dining out. Finally one of these families asked to adopt him, journalists Lauren Martin and Mike Seccombe with two small kids, Chiara and James. At this point the evil had been expunged and the Seccombes & their friends adored him until he died at the age of 18. At the bookstore, Beebe had in-and-out

privileges through the back door which made him quite the Cat About Town in the Campground. People would recognize him in the store and reveal they'd fed him this and that wonderful morsel, plus he'd spent the night on their porch. One afternoon I went out back to see a circle of young men blowing marijuana in Beebe's face. One of the guys looked up at me and said, "Dude, is this your cat?" as if they'd done this many times before. I brought Beebe inside and he performed a face plant into his dinner bowl.

I emailed my son Charlie, now 27, if he had anything to add about this cat of ours: "He was INSANE!" he wrote back.

PUFFIN

Leila & John McCarter

CHILMARK

There has never been, and will never be a more wonderful and beloved animal on this planet than Puffin, our Felinity.

— Leila

Puffin with Leila

DAISY & MACK

Ann Bassett & James Alley

WEST TISBURY

Sometimes one's relationship to cats is casual. Daisy is intense.

—Ann

Daisy

Mack

Mack with James

WINNIE & ELLA

Lesley Segal & Naomi Pallas

VINEYARD HAVEN

Winnie

Ella

LOLITA

Linda Alley

WEST TISBURY

Lolita is constantly talking, saying "HUMP" all the time. She loves to be vacuumed. Yes, with the electric vacuum cleaner, on her tummy and back and feet in particular.

COMPANIONS

Angelo is the great prince, like Aslan the great lion in
C. S. Lewis's books. He knows. He can read your thoughts.
He is my best friend.

—Jessie Benton

Kitty with George
(George Morgan page 26)

Poosa and Poose with Margaret

POOSE & POOSA • *Margaret Freydberg* • CHILMARK

A LETTER TO MY FAMILY, EXPLAINING
HOW I FEEL ABOUT MY CATS

Dearest family:

■ ■ ■

One day,
as I sat looking at my cats,
I felt a new, soft, opening space
around my armor-plate of rib cage –
like a warm wind
melting snow.
It was a feeling
of such sweet comfort,
there around my middle.
Breathing had another name.

Oh. But more than that.
For if unhappiness
feels like weights upon my chest,
and has the color of the night,
loving my cats
feels like the weights removed,
and daylight there.

■ ■ ■

It comes to me,
that what has made my looking,
loving,
is not the limbic lilt of seeing beauty,
though that is there.
It is the recognition
  of the character of a cat,
which is so anciently,
so perseveringly,
so unchangingly,
substantial –

Darwin's fittest.
In two white cats
I see the grace
of being what one knows one is,
and having it suffice eternally.

And I,
to be so old,
to be so new –
a luxurious lack of interest
  in the overlay of
me
on what it is I'm looking at,
lies now on me like
  loosened harnessing.
If breathing has another word,
then so does seeing.
I am focused on the knowing
  of a cat.

And so I end this letter
  to my family:

Come stay with me,
and be my loves.
Then I can love my cats
with temperance;
and all of you,
the way that watching
  two white cats
has taught me to.
　　　　—Margaret Freydberg

Excerpt from *Wanting -
New and Collected Poems*

Poosa

Bianca

ANGELO, BAFFI & BIANCA

Jessie Benton & Richard Guerin

CHILMARK, BOSTON, LOS ANGELES
& BAJA, MEXICO

What I would say about my princess Bianca is she is a mamma's girl, never leaves my side, talks softly about everything all the time, and thinks Angelo is the handsomest prince of all.

Baffi thinks he is invisible when he is in a shadow. He would like to think of himself as Balam, the great black jaguar of Mexico, but he is just a pile of black full of love fur.

Angelo is the great prince, like Aslan the great lion in C. S. Lewis's books. He knows. He can read your thoughts. He is my best friend.

—Jessie

Angelo

Bianca

Baffi

MOJO & PUTCY

Sam Eddy
CHILMARK

Jannette Vanderhoop
WEST TISBURY

Putcy with Sam

Mojo and Putcy with Jannette

DISCO & JASMINE

North Tabor Farm

Rebecca Miller & Matthew Dix
Sadie, Ruby & Joshua

CHILMARK

Jasmine

Disco with Ruby and Joshua

SIMBA, TOBY & NEFERTITI

Jessica Harris

OAK BLUFFS & BROOKLYN

Since I was a child, I have always had a black cat. There was Robespierre (Roby), followed by Obi, and just before she departed for graduate school, one of my students who had become a virtual daughter to me gave me Toby. He was, from the first, inquisitive, affectionate, and fearless in the manner of all kittens. I adore him! I have also always had Siamese cats as well. Here the legacy is too long to list, so after 21-year-old Askia and 22-year-old Mouss went to kitty Gloryland, Shaka and Simba came to join the household. They were tiny balls of fluff, all ears and rat tails, and I called them "wookies" from the Planet Rat until they grew into beautiful sleep beasties with hearts full of affection and throats full of purrs. Nefertiti was their sister and she was my mother's cat, although after my mother died in 2000, she gradually and grudgingly adopted me as second best.

Toby and Nefertiti had to be put to sleep 12 days apart last summer. I grieved for them like the family they were. Simba's still going strong at 15. Last fall, he was joined by a new all-black kitty who was adopted on Martha's Vineyard. He's feisty and still slightly feral and lets me pat him only when he feels like it. His adoptive name was Munchkin, but in my heart I know he's really Moby, the most recent in a line of fabulous black felines and the latest addition to my furry family.

Toby, Nefertiti and Simba

Nefertiti with Jessica

PHOEBE & ROSIE

Ann Hollister

VINEYARD HAVEN

My cats are my special companions.

Rosie

Rosie with Ann

Phoebe

SAUL

Ryan Malonson

AQUINNAH

Saul is His Highness.

SAMSON & DELILAH • *Doris Preston* • OAK BLUFFS & AGAWAM, MASS.

SUNSHINE

Emory Francis

AQUINNAH

MONA

Martha Fleishman

CHILMARK

She's my baby. I've had her forever.

KATIE & LUCY

Rev. Judy Campbell
& Christopher Stokes

OAK BLUFFS

Katie came to us as a surprise. We were looking for a cat, not a kitten. But there she was, the discarded one of a feral litter, and the rest is a delightful history. She has charmed us with her affection and faithful companionship. She's fond of sitting next to my computer and has, on occasion, been known to add to something I'm working on.

Lucy was a shy gentle tortoiseshell who took several years to find her voice. Once she did, she learned to use it well and to her advantage when it came to begging for treats. One of her favorite snoozing spots was in the dappled shade under a Japanese maple, where she was virtually invisible because of her natural camouflage.

—Judy

Katie and Lucy

Katie

Quinney and Ravee, the horse, with Liz

QUINNEY & QUITSA • *Liz & Steve Lewenberg* • CHILMARK

LOTS OF CATS

Fourteen cats! Every day we say how blessed we are since everyone gets along so well.

—Susan Jones

Nell and kittens Butch, Bella & Bingo with Tessa Dahl

ALFRED, PERDY, MILO, HARRY, NELL & KITTENS: BINGO, BELLA & BUTCH

Tessa Dahl
Patricia Neal

VINEYARD HAVEN

They all have "lion cuts" like poodles except the kittens who are too young.

Alfred

Bingo and Bella

Harry

Perdy

Milo

Nell with Patricia

145

FRECKLE, LION, BABY PUFF & BENNY

Lori Pinkham & Kyle Amaral
Riley, Zander, Kylee & Skyler

VINEYARD HAVEN

Baby Puff and Freckle

Freckle with Lori and Skyler

Freckle, Lion and Baby Puff with Zander, Riley and Skyler

ANGEL, LIMA BEAN, RALPH, RAVEN, SCOOBY, WATSON, KIPLING, ANNABELLE, SQUIRREL, THOMAS, EARLY, ELI, ROOSTER COGBURN & WOODY

Susan Jones & Bruce Yauney

VINEYARD HAVEN & CHILMARK

Fourteen cats! Every day we say how blessed we are since everyone gets along so well.

We have all of our cats because nobody wanted them.

Having worked with animal rescue groups in New Jersey, Connecticut, and Massachusetts, I've seen firsthand what happens without responsible pet care. Here on the Vineyard, thanks to groups like P.A.W.S. (Pet Adoption and Welfare Service), Cattrap and Helping Homeless Animals, homeless cats can receive medical care, spaying and neutering, socialization and a chance at a loving home.

—Susan

Angel and Lima Bean

Lima Bean, Watson and Eli with Susan

148

Kipling

Eli

Rooster Cogburn

Angel

Woody

Lima Bean and Rooster Cogburn

149

ZIP, LIAM, SCULLY, MIDNIGHT, PEARL & FISH

Sandy & Steve Atwood, VMD

WEST TISBURY

I know that you are not supposed to have a favorite but my little buddy Liam really is my favorite. Every night at bedtime he zooms up the stairs, jumps on the bed and wants to be patted indefinitely before we both fall asleep. It's hard falling asleep without him!

—Steve

Fish

Liam

Midnight

Pearl

Liam, Midnight, Scully and Fish with Sandy and Steve

CATTRAP ◆ *Lee Dubin, 40+ Cats* ◆ WEST TISBURY

Cattrap is dedicated to the mission to spay and neuter homeless feral cats on Martha's Vineyard. Established in 1999, it is also a farm sanctuary for cats, located in West Tisbury on fifteen acres. The cats are housed, fed, and given medical treatment if needed—all supported by private charitable donations.

MARTHA'S VINEYARD
HELPING HOMELESS ANIMALS, INC.
(2010 – CURRENT)

Kym Cyr

OAK BLUFFS

Formerly, Second Chance Animal Rescue, MVHHA is a non-profit, cage-free, no-kill animal rescue shelter that provides medical, physical and emotional needs to homeless animals while finding permanent homes.

MSPCA ANIMAL CARE & ADOPTION CENTER (1933-2009)

Ronald Whitney, Manager (1978-2009)

EDGARTOWN

The MSPCA of Martha's Vineyard (1933 – 2009) began as the Katherine Foote memorial shelter. It took in abandoned animals and arranged adoptions in new homes.

Daphne with Ronald

ANIMAL SHELTER OF MARTHA'S VINEYARD ◆ *Lisa Hayes, Shelter Manager* ◆ EDGARTOWN

The Animal Shelter was established in May 2009 after the MSPCA discontinued its services on Martha's Vineyard.
Its mission is to provide shelter, health care, love and support to most domestic animals until a permanent home is found.

SURVIVORS

*She used to be the sweetest kitten – then she had a couple
of litters and a really HARD birth, really scary. I brought her in
to get her spayed after the second litter and lo and behold,
she was pregnant. Another hard birth for her.*

—*Janet Messineo*

Phoebe

PHOEBE

Janet Messineo & Tristan Israel
VINEYARD HAVEN

I can hardly believe that Phoebe is 21 going on 22 years old. She is a little pistol! She used to be the sweetest kitten – then she had a couple of litters and a really HARD birth, really scary. I brought her in to get her spayed after the second litter and lo and behold, she was pregnant. Another hard birth for her. Poor thing. After she was spayed I don't know what happened. Hormones? she became such a bitch. If I got too close to her she would whack me, or anyone. You could not pick her up, she would scratch your face. When she was about in her teens, she started to have seizures. She was on Phenobarbital for quite a few years but had not had a seizure in a looonng time. I weaned her off the meds and she has been fine until last week she had a seizure. I just put her back on the meds. BUT she is eating like a pig, letting the dogs Lina and Pepe know who is BOSS, comes on walks in the woods with us and full of piss and vinegar. At this rate she might live to be 25 or more.

—Janet

MARIA TERESA

Carmine Cerone

VINEYARD HAVEN

We've had lots of cats…like the survivors that they are, they find us…walk in the door; get left to us by others; are inherited; beg for rescue. Diego, Raoul, Riccardo, Maria Consuela, Maria Teresa and Jean Pierre (a Paris street urchin).

Our current Maria Teresa was rescued after the demise of her sister Maria Consuela, a real survivor who used up all her nine lives. The runt of a litter, Maria was saved from drowning by some exchange students living in our building. When they left to go back to Europe, of course we were required to adopt her. We were summering on the Vineyard then and fortunate enough to be spending a couple of years in Paris.

Maria Consuela disappeared just before we were about to leave the Vineyard – much searching, wrenching of hands and hearts, but we had to leave for Paris without Maria C. Lots of prayers and six weeks later, after our hopes were waning, a call from Dr. Steve that Maria C. had been found. Through the efforts of several wonderful Vineyard friends, she was Cape Air'ed to Boston and put on an Air France jet to Paris. She arrived at the DeGaulle freight terminal in her pink carrier, skinny, with health problems, and on the last of her nine lives, we thought. But there were still some lives left in her. She happily enjoyed another 10 years. Each cat has its story… we look forward to the next one to cross our threshold.

KITTY

Alison Mead

OAK BLUFFS

Kitty was abandoned in a cardboard box on a frigid December evening outside the Kmart in Jackson, Wyoming, where I was living at the time. She was tiny and scared, barely over a month old. When no one at the store volunteered, I offered to take her home for just the night. Too little for big jumps, she cried at the foot of the bed until I scooped her up and put her on my pillow. She snuggled into my neck where she slept all night long. By morning it was clear that she wasn't going anywhere. I made it my mission to make her feel loved and wanted every day of her life.

For 14 years Kitty's been by my side for all kinds of adventures: cross-country road trips, two degree programs, relationships, career changes. More often than not, the question I'm asked after "How are you?" is "How is Kitty?" Everyone knows that she means the world to me, and I mean the world to her. We're inseparable. Kitty's getting older now and with that come health issues. Two years ago she was diagnosed with diabetes. After a month of insulin shots, she miraculously went into remission. Now, she has kidney disease. We tried iv fluid treatments, but the stress on each of us, and our relationship, was too much. She has a hard time jumping up on the bed sometimes now, just like when she was a kitten, so I've put a little stool beside the bed to make it easier for her. And still, every night, just like that first night in Wyoming, she shares my pillow as we drift off to sleep. I used to think I saved her, but the truth is we saved each other.

ChiChi with Lucinda

CHICHI, MAXIE & SALLY

Lucinda Sheldon

OAK BLUFFS

As for ChiChi, she was born in St. Thomas. Her mother was all black, and her father pure Siamese. She was abandoned along with her twin brother, and I found her at the shelter being nursed by another mother cat with her own litter. She and her brother Ti were only about five weeks old when I found them, and because they were putting such stress on the mother cat, I was able to adopt them both when they were about six weeks. My son Jesse nurtured Ti and I nurtured ChiChi. We would take them to bed with us to keep them warm and safe. Unfortunately wild dogs killed Ti and two other cats of mine, so ChiChi was the true survivor. We moved here in 1995, when she was almost four years old. I truly think she knew I had saved her, that was why she was so devoted.

Maxie

Maxie

Sally

163

YOLANDA

Doug Kent
WEST TISBURY

My daughter Lizzy adopted Yo Yo after the cat's mother was struck by a car and died. Lizzy hand-fed Yo Yo and made her the wonderful cat she is today. When Yo Yo was two years old, Lizzy went off to LA to study and work, leaving the cat with her mother, Lesley. Several months later there was a very bad fire at the house. Yo Yo had a way to come and go through the basement. During the fire she should have left the house, but instead she raced up stairs where the fire was and went to Lesley's room where she was sleeping and screeched several times. Lesley woke up and was able to race down the stairs, scorching her hair.

Later, when Lesley had to leave the house for a year, Lizzy asked if I would take Yo Yo. Right off we had a great bond. About six years later I unexpectedly had to stay in the hospital for a week, and made arrangements to have someone feed and check Yo Yo daily. However, one day she was off and gone. For six weeks after my return I posted signs, placed adds in the papers, drove to check sightings of black cats. Near the end of the six-week period I got a call from a woman opening a camp on James Pond. I had lived for a while near Seth's Pond and Yo Yo and I took long walks out in the woods near James Pond (about two miles from where we were living when she disappeared). I think she found her way back to where we took those long walks –that's where she must have been all this time – she went back to find me. She is the most wonderful companion I could have.

ROCKSTAR

Airport Laundromat
Nick Catt

WEST TISBURY

When she lived in Edgartown, Rockstar returned home one day badly injured and missing her long fluffy tail. Vet Steve Atwood performed surgery and she has completely recovered, but no tail. A survivor!

She has the best life of any cat: climbs more trees, spends most of her day outside, comes in at night, sleeps at the laundromat. Rockstar has many admirers who come to visit her.

Rockstar with Colleen, a visitor

Crowd with Sydney

BABY BUCK & CROWD

Michelle Jasny, VMD & Max Jasny
Lila & Sydney
WEST TISBURY

December 3, 1990. My neighbor Doug is hunting in the State Forest. It's cold. There's snow on the ground. What's that huddled in the middle of the path? A kitten. A very tiny kitten. "I named her Buckshot," he says an hour later, handing me the bundle of shivering black fur. "Because she looked like a bit of shot in the snow." Skin and bones, Buckshot weighs a mere 1.3 pounds, has 104.7 fever, and is trembling violently. "Hard to tell at this point what her chances are," I sigh. She is obviously sick, malnourished, and suffering from exposure. "Do what you can," Doug says.

"Buckshot?" Beth (my assistant) sputtered. "What kind of name is that? We'll call you Baby Buckshot." Baby Buckshot it was. Baby baby baby baby Buck, we crooned. Six days after arriving, Buck began eating on her own. By late December she weighed a whopping two pounds and could walk across the room. Although her head still trembled, especially when eating, she was undeniably ready to go home. Only I couldn't let her go. You may know that feeling. The way one special animal inexplicably steals your heart. That one particular dog or cat that you love beyond reason. A bit sheepishly, I called Doug. "You weren't really looking for a cat..." I started.

Nineteen years later, I have lived with Baby Buck longer than any other creature, including parents, husband, or children. When I was starting my

Baby Buck, Sydney, Lila and Michelle

practice, she graced my desk while I did paperwork late at night, struggling alone to make ends meet. When a pregnant stray cat gave birth here, Buck attended. Later she babysat, letting the kittens pretend-nurse on her while the mother cat took a break. Three of the kittens stayed permanently and Buck mothered them for the rest of their lives, outliving them all. When I suffered multiple miscarriages, Baby Buck curled up with me in bed, nose to nose, rubbing her face against my cheek, as though wiping away my tears. And always, I held her in my arms, crooning "babybabybabybabybuck."

Michelle Jasny from "VisitingVet," *The Martha's Vineyard Times*, Dec. 17, 2009

KIKI, KOKO, KUMQUAT, MIMI & MONKEY

Trish Ing & David Wiley

EDGARTOWN

Every morning when they do an hour of meditation, Mimi sits for the full hour in David's lap. She had cancer on her ears four years ago, had it removed, and the fur never grew back. She has to have sunblock on those areas in the summertime.

All our cats are rescues from Queens, New York.

— Trish

Mimi with Trish

Mimi

Kumquat

Kiki

MARCEL

Brigitte Cornand

WEST TISBURY, NEW YORK CITY & PARIS

Marcel is a New York tiger: beautiful paws, large stripes and strong claws. And of course splendid eyes. I met him in December 2010. At that time I was still mourning my beloved Siamese Petit Loup ("little wolf" in English) thinking: I'll never adopt another cat, it's too hard and too sad when they go away. By chance this morning I had to bring back some things to my vet at a huge hospital in Chelsea with a cat adoption department. When I looked at the cages, an enormous cat moved slowly near me and meowed gently. "Carlos loves you," said the receptionist. "In general he never talks!" I immediately read the note next to him, which said: "I'm here for almost two years, my parents abandoned me after losing their jobs. My vet is very nice but now I really would love to have Christmas in a family." I burst into tears – and now we have lived together since December 24, 2010. His new name is Marcel because of Marcel Duchamp and every day it's enchanting.

DINAH ◆ *Faith & Hasty Runner* ◆ WEST TISBURY

When we found Dinah at the MSPCA she was so fat, she had squeezed herself inside a shoe-box, so fat she draped over the sides. She refused to look at anybody, poor thing; she'd given up hope. There were some beautiful other cats there, but we fastened on Dinah because she was so tragic but proud. The minute she got in the car she seemed to feel better. When we brought her home she was so happy. She threw herself down on the bed in ecstasy. So glad to have a home.

PUCCINI ◆ *Rainbow Farm, Laura Campbell* ◆ CHILMARK

Puccini spent her first seven years on a farm in upstate New York. After she was attacked by a bull terrier and suffered a broken back when thrown out of a car, Laura Campbell rescued her and brought her back to live at Rainbow Farm in Chilmark.

—L.C.

IN MEMORY

I want you to know that they will tell you,
you will know when the time is right.
Cats are so special they will never let you down.

—*Joe Barkett*

Romeo

ADAY, ELLA & ROMEO • *Rachel Fox* • CHILMARK & NEW YORK CITY

Romeo was severely neglected by his original owner. After finding him roaming around 72nd St. for the fourth time and with a torn ear, a friend who lived in his building told the owner she wouldn't return him if she found him again. At midnight before a job interview, my friend called to say that she had found him again and was bringing him over. He hid under the bed for the first few days, but shortly thereafter became the most loving pet I've ever known and one of the most trusting. He could make cat lovers of plumbers and repairmen whose first comment on entering was "keep

Ella

Aday

those animals away from me." Although Abyssinians are an intelligent breed, Romeo's intelligence was almost human. After watching me in the bathroom, he started using the toilet instead of the litter box. Once, after catching a mouse, my friend pulled out a box and said, "Romy, put him in the box." He marched over proudly, dropped the mouse in the box, turned around and walked away. My former boyfriend said that Romeo would rest his head on his paws, staring adoringly at me while I slept, purring. If I turned over in my sleep and happened to face him, the purring was so loud that it could be heard—like a motor—in the next room, "as if the sun had just risen and was shining on Romeo's face." He slept either draped over me or with his back pressed up against me, stretched to his full length so that as much of his body as possible was touching mine. When I would pick him up and say "hugs," he would throw his arms around my neck. He sat on my shoulder like a parrot or draped like a scarf while I worked at the computer. He talked to the pigeons on

the window ledge and to all of the animals climbing in the trees, on the ground and around the house at the Vineyard. He was a happy guy. I miss him every day.

I named Ella after Ella Fitzgerald because she was always talking in a very melodic voice, singing. Like her namesake, she was tremendously lovable and a great eater. She had beautiful eyes and she loved to listen to music.

I found Aday on the street in Newark, New Jersey in 2000, climbing around broken glass on the site of a demolished building – skin and bones. I bought some chicken at a Popeye's Restaurant and pulled off the fried part; she ate the meat with such enthusiasm that she drew blood from one of my fingers. When she finished, someone opened the door to the Popeye's and she flew in at lightning speed, jumping from table to table, stealing chicken from customers' plates. She has always been a tough gal. If you try to shut her out of a room, she will stand at the door and cry "Huh-WOH?" and it sounds just like "hello."

TWEEDS

Diana & Whit Manter

WEST TISBURY & BOSTON

Tweeds: 1991-2009

I was walking down my stone walkway towards my barn when I saw a flash of orange disappear through an old cat door. The house was on Upper Lambert's Cove Road down a narrow dirt road. There was land across the road I had fenced off where my horses roamed and a barn with two stalls of hay next to the house. I heard later that Tweeds had checked out other locations in the area but I guess she decided this was the one.

I closed all the doors, blocked off the cat door and started looking for her. I finally found her wedged between the planks of a hay pallet. I had to remove all the bales of hay but there she was: this little bit of a thing hiding. We figured her for three to six weeks old.

I left her in the barn, put out a cookie tray with some saw dust on it for litter, dry cat food and water. Every day she would eat, drink and use the litter but I never saw her unless I looked real hard. I would take her to the vets for shots, spaying etc, tucked into the front pocket of a Black Dog sweatshirt. I always brought her back to the barn and let her go again.

When it started getting cold another life long thing about Tweeds came out: she hated the cold. I finally found her buried behind the wood pile trying to stay warm and crying non stop. I brought her into the house, put down the litter and food, and she disappeared again. The house was old and had lots of holes and unfinished places. She could drop down into the basement without using a door or crawl back into the knee walls through openings. After two to three weeks of her using the litter, eating and drinking what I put out, I decided it was time. I crawled down a long knee wall, found her curled up in some insulation and brought her back into the house.

Little by little she became part of the family. She never took to other people and continued her life of hiding. At the moment she is dying of renal failure and she is hiding under the bathroom sink. We put her bed in there and she will die as she has lived in her own little space.

The only time I ever saw her play was with our cocker, Buff. Every morning Whit and I would wake up and Tweeds and Buff would be in the bed with us. I would say "Time to get up" and they would both jump out of bed and race for the stairway. They literally would be pushing each other out of the way, trying to get down first. I loved that.

—Diana

OTTO • *Betsy Corsiglia* • OAK BLUFFS

JASPURR

Joe Barkett

EDGARTOWN

I hate to tell you that my Jaspurr had to be put to sleep on July 7, his 19th birthday. I just had to do it; he had lost all of his muscle mass and was just failing quickly. He had a seizure a couple of months ago and Dr. Michelle Jasny and I knew that it was the brain tumor coming back. I had him barricaded in my living room after the seizure and as he revived some I could hear him at night breaking through. He finally made it up into my bed, even though he slipped off and I had to reach down and pull him up. It has been three years since the operation at Tufts. Michelle is the best, she just gave him hospice care and she and her staff were so supportive. I think that Jaspurr made the decision for me and I have to respect him for that and would expect no less from such a great cat. That night when I drove home it was the first time in 16 years that he was not there waiting for me. I could hardly get out of the car. I still catch myself looking for him. I still see him in the shadows.

I want you to know that they will tell you, you will know when the time is right. Cats are so special they will never let you down.

BEAR (1993-2011)

Tupelo Farm

WEST TISBURY

DIRECTORY

OF

101 CAT FAMILIES

BY TOWN

Bear
(Tupelo Farm page 184)

CATS OF AQUINNAH

CATS OF CHILMARK

CATS OF EDGARTOWN & CHAPPAQUIDDICK

CATS OF OAK BLUFFS

CATS OF VINEYARD HAVEN

CATS OF WEST TISBURY

IN MEMORY

James Alley
Despina and Barney Duane
Emory Francis
Bill Honey
Patricia Neal

CATS

Adagio
Baby Buck
Bear
Beebe
Miss Bianca
Britty
Brunhilda
Buck
Charlotte
ChiChi
Crowd
Dinah
Ella
Grace
Gus
Jaspurr
Kate Lin
Kiki
Kitty Brown
Koko
Kumquat

Lucy
Midnight
Mimi
Mojo
Monkey
Nefertiti
Otto
Pearl
Phoebe
Poose
Putcy
Quinney
Quitsa
Rainbow
Romeo
Simba
Toby
Tofu
Tweeds
Venice

Suzette

ACKNOWLEDGEMENTS

It takes an Island to make a book, or maybe two Islands. First and foremost I thank Cynthia Riggs for her encouragement and idea from the start for me to make a book about cats. To my special Wong family who gave me my first cats as well as my camera, love and thanks. I am grateful to all my patient friends-forever who listened, looked, read and spoke about the process, and egged me on. These include: Joanie Ames, Carmine Cerone, Shari Diamond, Catherine Finch, Fanny Howe, Kristen Kinser, Eileen Kitzis, Jonathan Revere, Jordan Ronson, Kathy Rose, Julia Smith, Bonnie & Fred Waitzkin and John Woodin. Francine Lynch, from the other Island, lent her valued support. Thanks to Cal Barksdale, my friend who remembers Priscilla on Lobsterville and all the cats after her – I'm grateful for his professional editorial eye. Susanna Sturgis gave the text her meticulous copyedit. Many thanks to Janet Holladay of Tisbury Printer for her steady coaching on book matters and design. Special thanks to Jane McTeigue for lending her creative skills and spirit to the final stages. Jan Pogue gave her expert book direction for print and marketing concerns. And of course, much appreciation to the 101 cat people in this book who shared their wonderful stories – each one unique – to create our special Vineyard family tale.